The *Let's-Read-and-Find-Out Science* book series was originated by Dr. Franklyn M. Branley, Astronomer Emeritus and former Chairman of the American Museum–Hayden Planetarium, and was formerly co-edited by him and Dr. Roma Gans, Professor Emeritus of Childhood Education, Teachers College, Columbia University. Text and illustrations for each book in the series are checked for accuracy by an expert in the relevant field. For a complete catalog of Let's-Read-and-Find-Out Science books, write to HarperCollins Children's Books, 10 East 53rd Street, New York, NY 10022.

Library of Congress Cataloging-in-Publication Data
Aliki.
  Digging up dinosaurs.
  (Let's-read-and-find-out science. Stage 2)
  Summary: Briefly introduces various types of dinosaurs whose
skeletons and reconstructions are seen in museums and explains
how scientists uncover, preserve, and study fossilized dinosaur
bones.
  ISBN 0-690-04714-2.—ISBN 0-690-04716-9 (lib. bdg.)
  ISBN 0-06-445078-3 (pbk.)
  1. Dinosaurs—Juvenile literature. [1. Dinosaurs. 2. Fossils]
I. Title.
QE862.D5A34   1988   567.9′1   87-29949
                     Revised Edition
      10 11 12 13 SCP 20 19 18 17 16 15 14 13 12 11

for Beverly Kobrin

DIGGING UP DINOSAURS

Have you ever seen dinosaur skeletons in a museum?

I have.

I visit them all the time.

I went again yesterday.

I saw APATOSAURUS.

I saw CORYTHOSAURUS.

I saw IGUANODON and TRICERATOPS.
I like to say their names.

SCOLOSAURUS was just where I had left it.
And TYRANNOSAURUS REX looked as fierce as ever.
TYRANNOSAURUS used to scare me.
I still can't believe how big it is.
Just its head is almost twice my size.

I'm not afraid of dinosaurs anymore.
Sometimes I call them "you bag of bones"
   under my breath.
I can spend hours looking at them.
I used to wonder where they came from
   and how they got into the museum.
But now I know.

I'm scared.

Here he is!

One swat of his tail would show you how *little*.

This is a little fella.

9

Dinosaurs lived millions of years ago.

A few of them were as small as birds,

   but most were enormous.

Some dinosaurs ate plants.

Some dinosaurs ate the meat of other dinosaurs.

And some may even have eaten the eggs of other dinosaurs.

Dinosaurs lived almost everywhere on Earth.

They lived for millions of years.

Then they died out.

No one is sure why they became extinct.

But they did.

There hasn't been a dinosaur around for

   65 million years.

DIPLODOCUS

BRACHIOSAURUS

COMPSOGNATHUS

ORNITHOMIMUS

TYRANNOSAURUS

11

Until about 200 years ago, no one knew
   anything about dinosaurs.
Then people began finding things in rock.
They found large footprints.
They found huge, mysterious bones
   and strange teeth.
People were finding fossils.
They began asking questions about them.

Fossils are a kind of diary of the past.

They are the remains of plants and animals that died long ago.

Instead of rotting or crumbling away, the remains
were preserved, and slowly turned to stone.

Fossil hunters found more and more big bones
in different parts of the world.
Scientists studied the fossils.
They said the bones and teeth and footprints
all belonged to a group of giant reptiles
that lived on Earth for millions of years.
The giants were named DINOSAURIA, or terrible lizards.

1822

Mary Ann Mantell found the first dinosaur fossils, in England. She discovered some giant fossil teeth.

1825

Her husband, Dr. Gideon Mantell, named the animal IGUANODON, or Iguana-Tooth.

Nine years later, he found a mass of IGUANODON bones.

1841

Dr. Richard Owen named the giant reptiles DINOSAURIA.

What finds these were!

People crowded into museums to see them.

But the dinosaur bones didn't just get up and walk there.

They had to be dug out of the ground, slowly and patiently.

Even today, digging up dinosaurs is not an easy job.
A team of experts must work together.

PALEONTOLOGIST
A scientist who studies ancient plants and animals.

GEOLOGIST
A scientist who can tell the age of rocks and fossils.

DRAFTSMAN
who draws pictures of the fossils.

WORKERS
who dig the fossil
out of the rock.

PHOTOGRAPHER
who takes pictures
of the find.

SPECIALISTS
who prepare the
fossil for the
museum.

17

This is how fossil hunters work.

First, they have to find a dinosaur.

They search along riverbanks and in quarries.

They climb up high cliffs and down into steep canyons.

With luck, someone spots a fossil bone
poking through the rock.

The site is covered with a tent, and the work begins.

Sometimes the fossil is buried so deep, the rock
   around it has to be drilled or blasted.

Tons of rubble are carted away.

Scientists chip at the rock close to the fossil.

They brush away the grit.

They have to be very careful.

As soon as a bone is uncovered,
it is brushed with shellac.
The shellac helps hold the bone together,
so it won't crumble.
Then the bone is numbered.

Sometimes a skeleton has to be cut apart
so that it can be moved.
The draftsman draws each bone in its
exact position, and the photographer
takes pictures.
That way, there can be no mix-up later,
when someone tries to put the skeleton
together.

21

When the bones are ready to be moved,
they are carefully wrapped.
Small bones are wrapped in tissue paper
and put into boxes or sacks.

Large bones are left half buried in the rock.
They will be dug out later, in the museum.
These fossils are covered with a plaster cast,
    just as a broken leg is.

First, the parts of the fossil that show are covered with wet tissue paper, and then with strips of burlap dipped in wet plaster. Then the whole piece is wrapped in the same way. When the plaster dries, it becomes very hard. The tissue-paper covering makes the cast easier to remove later.

Each bone is then packed in straw, put into a crate,
and taken to the museum.

At the museum, scientists unwrap the fossil.

They finish digging it out of the rock.

They study the bone.

This rock is 115 million years old. That means the dinosaur is, too.

I can tell from these many flat teeth that this was a plant eater.

Scientists dig out the fossil in many different ways. They use a hammer and chisel, fine needles, power tools that work like a dentist's drill, special sandblasting machines, and even chemicals that dissolve the rock but do not harm the fossil.

They compare the bones to other dinosaur bones.
They compare them to the bones of other animals.
They try to figure out what size and shape the dinosaur was.
They try to find out how the dinosaur stood
and walked, and what it ate.

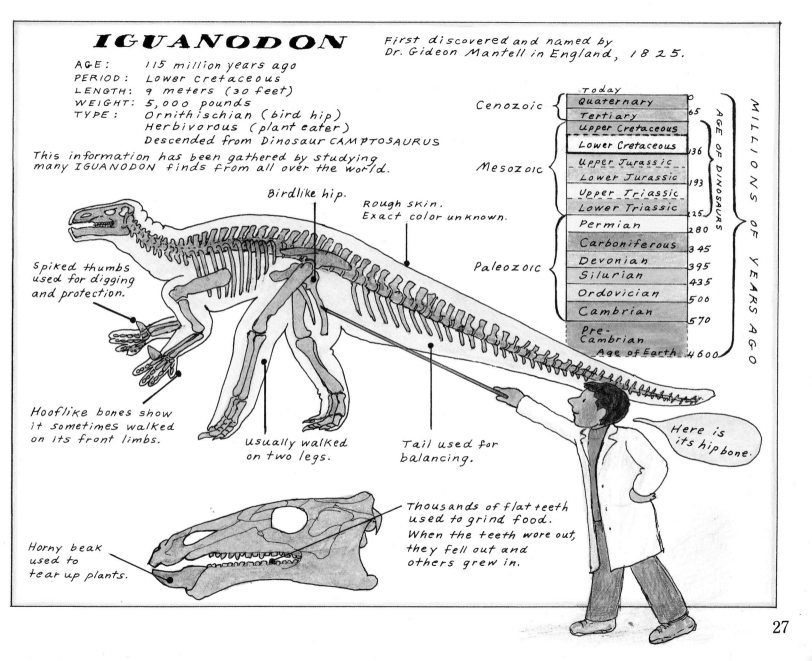

IGUANODON

First discovered and named by
Dr. Gideon Mantell in England, 1825.

AGE: 115 million years ago
PERIOD: Lower Cretaceous
LENGTH: 9 meters (30 feet)
WEIGHT: 5,000 pounds
TYPE: Ornithischian (bird hip)
Herbivorous (plant eater)
Descended from Dinosaur CAMPTOSAURUS

This information has been gathered by studying
many IGUANODON finds from all over the world.

Birdlike hip.

Rough skin.
Exact color unknown.

Spiked thumbs
used for digging
and protection.

Hooflike bones show
it sometimes walked
on its front limbs.

Usually walked
on two legs.

Tail used for
balancing.

Here is
its hip bone.

Horny beak
used to
tear up plants.

Thousands of flat teeth
used to grind food.
When the teeth wore out,
they fell out and
others grew in.

		MILLIONS OF YEARS AGO
Cenozoic	Today	
	Quaternary	0
	Tertiary	65
Mesozoic	Upper Cretaceous	
	Lower Cretaceous	136
	Upper Jurassic	
	Lower Jurassic	193
	Upper Triassic	
	Lower Triassic	225
Paleozoic	Permian	280
	Carboniferous	345
	Devonian	395
	Silurian	435
	Ordovician	500
	Cambrian	570
	Pre-Cambrian	
	Age of Earth	4600

AGE OF DINOSAURS

If there are enough bones, scientists are able
to build a complete skeleton.
A frame is made in the shape of the dinosaur
to support the bones.
The bones are wired together, one by one.
They are held in place with pieces of metal.
If any bones are missing, plastic or fiberglass ones
are made to replace them.
You can hardly tell the new bones from the old ones.

After many months the work is complete.
The dinosaur skeleton looks just as it once did.

29

Until recently, only a few museums had dinosaurs.

Then scientists learned how to make copies of the skeletons.

The copy is hard to make.

It takes a long time.

The original skeleton has to be taken completely
apart, bone by bone.

A mold is made for each bone.

The new pieces are made of fiberglass.

A fiberglass dinosaur is just as scary as the original,
but much stronger and lighter.

The original bone is covered with rubber latex and an outer coating of fiberglass, to hold the rubber stiff. This is peeled off the bone to form the mold. The inside of the mold is brushed with resin and filled with fiberglass. Many dinosaurs can be made from the same molds.

Now museums all over the world have dinosaur skeletons.
And many people can spend hours looking at them,
the way I do.